REHAB or PUNISHMENT:
What to Do About Drug Crimes

Carla Mooney

ReferencePoint Press®

San Diego, CA

© 2020 ReferencePoint Press, Inc.
Printed in the United States

For more information, contact:
ReferencePoint Press, Inc.
PO Box 27779
San Diego, CA 92198
www.ReferencePointPress.com

LIBRARY OF CONGRESS CATALOGING-IN-PUBLICATION DATA

Name: Mooney, Carla, author.
Title: Rehab or Punishment: What to Do About Drug Crimes/by Carla Mooney.
Description: San Diego, CA: ReferencePoint Press, Inc., 2020.
Identifiers: LCCN 2019007517 (print) | LCCN 2019009951 (ebook) | ISBN
  9781682827406 (eBook) | ISBN 9781682827390 (hardback)
Subjects: LCSH: Drug traffic—United States. | Drug control—United States. |
  Drug abuse and crime—United States. | Criminals—Rehabilitation—United
  States.
Classification: LCC HV5801 (ebook) | LCC HV5801 .M6635 2020 (print) | DDC
  364.60973—dc23
LC record available at https://lccn.loc.gov/2019007517

CONTENTS

PUNISH OR REHABILITATE?

Bernard Noble was released from a Louisiana prison in 2018 after serving seven years for possession of about two joints worth of marijuana. Under the state's habitual offender law, Noble had been sentenced to thirteen years of hard labor without possibility of parole. Despite past convictions, all of which involved having small amounts of cocaine or marijuana, his case became a symbol of the nation's harsh drug laws and sentencing practices. Noble's reprieve resulted from efforts by lawyers and others who argued that his sentence was out of line with laws in various states that now classify small amounts of marijuana as legal. In 2015 Louisiana lawmakers had even passed a bill that reduced maximum sentences for marijuana possession, including for multiple convictions.

Noble, who was granted parole, is one of many people nationwide who have served or are currently serving long sentences for nonviolent drug offenses. Federal and many state laws have long required mandatory minimum sentences for drug crimes. Noble believes that the criminal justice system needs to change how it deals with people who are caught with small amounts of drugs. "I'm not perfect, not many of us are, and I have had my challenges in life," Noble said before his release. "But we live in a country where we would like to believe that all life is precious, and to destroy a life and take someone's freedom for 13 years for a tiny amount of marijuana is so overkill. I have no violent past. . . . I take full responsibility for my actions. . . . The pain I have caused with my incarceration to my family is the cross I bear."[1]

The First Step Act

Changes are coming. In December 2018 Congress passed and President Donald Trump signed into law a sweeping criminal justice reform bill called the First Step Act. The act modifies federal sentencing laws, including shortening mandatory minimum sentences for nonviolent drug offenders. It allows judges more discretion to consider individual circumstances and facts if they do not believe that the mandatory minimum sentence is appropriate. The new law also allows drug offenders sentenced before 2010 to petition for their cases to be reevaluated. This reevaluation could reduce the sentences of thousands of drug offenders who are serving long sentences for crack cocaine offenses (which have usually resulted in harsher penalties than for similar drugs). Additionally, the law expands job training and other programs designed to reduce recidivism rates, which are the rates at which convicted criminals commit new crimes.

"We live in a country where we would like to believe that all life is precious, and to destroy a life and take someone's freedom for 13 years for a tiny amount of marijuana is so overkill."[1]

—Bernard Noble, convicted drug offender

Many of the changes in the First Step Act are modeled after reforms implemented by a handful of states, including Texas, Kansas, Ohio, and South Carolina. The goal of those reforms is to reduce costs and improve outcomes of the criminal justice system. Although the First Step Act only affects those sentenced in federal courts, supporters hope that it will become a model for more state-level criminal justice reforms. This matters because most drug crimes are state and not federal crimes.

Under the new law, thousands of federal inmates are now eligible for sentence reductions and early release programs. Going forward, the act will benefit new offenders by allowing reduced sentences. It will also shift the emphasis from punishment to helping people lead lawful, productive lives after release. "We're not just talking about money. We're talking about human potential," said Texas senator John Cornyn on the Senate floor in December

2018. "We're investing in the men and women who want to turn their lives around once they're released from prison, and we're investing in . . . stronger and more viable communities."[2]

Increasing Debate

In recent years, the issue of how to most effectively deal with drug crimes has been increasingly debated. Historical thinking that harsh punishment best deters crime has led to tough-on-crime laws and sentencing. An increasing number of people believe that harsh prison and sentencing laws have created a criminal justice system that is expensive and unfair while doing little to reduce recidivism and make communities safer.

The First Step Act signals a change in thinking about how to address crimes involving drugs. Research has shown that many people who are in prison for drug crimes are addicts. For these

Surrounded by criminal justice reformers and members of Congress, President Donald Trump signs the First Step Act in December 2018. The act modifies sentencing guidelines for nonviolent drug offenders.

people, addiction treatment and rehabilitation may be more effective than long prison sentences at helping them turn their lives around and stay out of the criminal justice system. States that have already started making these types of changes are experiencing good results. According to Cornyn, sentencing and prison reforms in Texas have had positive outcomes. "We've seen these changes implemented across the country at the state level, including my home state of Texas, which have yielded incredible results," he says. "So using [the] sorts of recidivism reduction programs that are included in the First Step Act at the state level, we were able to reduce our incarceration rate and our crime rate by double-digits at the same time."[3]

Recent polls suggest that Americans today generally favor treatment, rehab, and other alternatives over long prison sentences for non-violent drug offenders. A 2017 poll by the American Civil Liberties Union (ACLU), for instance, found that 71 percent of Americans do not see long prison sentences as an effective way to improve public safety. This group also believes that such sentences might even increase the likelihood that an offender will commit another crime, because prisons do not do a good job of rehabilitating inmates with drug addiction and other issues. "Our poll demonstrates near-consensus support for criminal justice reform, including reducing the prison population, reinvesting in rehabilitation and treatment, and eliminating policies like mandatory minimums. Americans believe that resources should be shifted from incarceration to rehabilitation,"[4] says the ACLU's Udi Ofer.

"Americans believe that resources should be shifted from incarceration to rehabilitation."[4]

—Udi Ofer, deputy national political director and Campaign for Smart Justice director at the ACLU

As the debate over how to address crimes involving drugs continues, more communities are considering criminal justice reforms. While some people still support tough-on-crime policies and harsh punishments for these crimes, others believe that implementing policies to make rehabilitation a priority is a more effective way to build better communities for the future.

SERVING TIME FOR DRUG CRIMES

Prisons in the United States are filled with people who have violated drug laws. One in five incarcerated people is locked up for a drug offense, according to a March 2019 report from the Prison Policy Initiative, a criminal justice public policy think tank. In Pennsylvania, for instance, 13,708 people were incarcerated for drug crimes as of December 31, 2017, a number that is 28.3 percent of the state's total inmates. In Kentucky in January 2018, 4,713 people were incarcerated for drug crimes—20 percent of the state's inmate population. In all, about 198,000 drug offenders were in state prisons in 2018.

In addition to state prisons, local jails and federal prisons also house drug offenders. According to the Prison Policy Initiative's March 2019 report, local jails hold about thirty-five thousand convicted drug offenders. An additional eighty-one thousand people were serving time for drug crimes in federal prisons, according to the report. Another few thousand are serving time in youth and military correctional facilities.

Twenty-one-year-old Amanuel Hagos is one example of a drug offender who is serving time in prison. In December 2017 Hagos was arrested and charged in Loveland, Colorado, with felony drug possession with the intent to distribute and felony drug possession with a weapon. He pleaded guilty to the charges. In October 2018 a judge sentenced Hagos to serve sixteen years in prison. At the sentencing hearing, the deputy district attorney characterized Hagos as having a recurring problem with drug abuse, and the judge noted that a combination of drugs, drug dealing, and violent behavior had led Hagos to this point. Although every case is different, these are common elements of many drug crimes.

Drug Offenders in Prison

Most drug offenders in state prisons and local jails are serving time for drug possession, but other crimes are also common. Some have been convicted of drug dealing or possession with the intent to distribute. Other offenders are serving time for the manufacture of drugs.

In the federal system the majority of drug convictions are related to drug trafficking, which is the illegal sale and distribution of a controlled substance. Drug trafficking generally involves large quantities of illegal substances. According to the most recent figures available from the US Department of Justice (DOJ), more than half of drug offenders in federal prison (54 percent) committed crimes involving cocaine.

People of every race, gender, and age are in prison for drug offenses. In the federal system the race of drug offenders varied by drug type—88 percent of crack cocaine offenders were African American, 54 percent of powder cocaine offenders were Latino, and 48 percent of methamphetamine offenders were white, DOJ statistics show. Overall across all drug types, 21.8 percent of offenders were white, 38.8 percent were African American, and 37.2 percent were Hispanic or Latino. Federal drug offenders were also heavily male (92.5 percent) and aged thirty-nine or younger (62.6 percent), according to the DOJ report.

Punishment for drug crimes often depends on whether the offender is charged in the state or federal system. Federal laws apply when a drug crime occurs on federal land, such as a military base or Washington, DC. Federal laws also apply if any part of the drug crime involves multiple states or crosses international borders. The primary difference between federal and state drug laws is the severity of punishment after conviction. Drug crimes convicted in federal court generally carry harsher punishments and longer sentences.

Drug offenders in both state and federal prisons are on average spending more time in prison than in the past. According to a 2018 Pew Charitable Trusts research report, inmates in state prisons serve an average of 2.2 years behind bars for drug offenses—a 36 percent increase over 1990. In federal prisons, the increase is even larger. Federal drug offenders spend an average of 5 years in prison, as compared to 2 years in 1998. Longer sentences for drug crimes are the result of laws implemented since the 1980s.

Inmates run in an enclosed prison exercise yard in Utah. People of every race, gender, and age are in prison for drug offenses.

Addicted Behind Bars

Many of those incarcerated for drug-related offenses have a substance abuse problem. A Bureau of Justice Statistics report released in 2017 states that 21 percent of people in state prisons and local jails are incarcerated because they committed crimes to support a drug habit. While some of these inmates are in jail for drug crimes like possession or trafficking, others are in prison for other types of crimes. Almost 40 percent of inmates serving time for property crimes and 14 percent of those incarcerated for violent crimes report that they committed their most serious offense for drug-related reasons. These include committing a violent offense while under the influence of drugs and committing a crime to get money to pay for drugs.

Also, the report found that more than half of state prison inmates and two-thirds of the sentenced jail population report that they have a drug dependence or abuse problem, as compared to 5 percent of the general adult population. Also, almost 40 percent of inmates in state prisons and jails report that they were using drugs at the time they committed the offense for which they were incarcerated. "We know for a vast majority of them, if it was not for their addiction, they wouldn't be in our facility,"[5] says Chris Pirolli, the director of corrections in Bucks County, Pennsylvania.

"We know for a vast majority of them, if it was not for their addiction, they wouldn't be in our facility."[5]

—Chris Pirolli, the director of corrections in Bucks County, Pennsylvania

Outcomes Vary

One of the goals of sending people to prison for any type of crime, including drug crimes, is to deter future crime and provide them with rehabilitation services to help them become law-abiding citizens upon their release. However, for inmates serving time for drug crimes who are also struggling with addiction, the outcomes vary. Some are able to turn their lives around, while others continue to cycle in and out of prison.

Larry Jasper is one of the success stories. In 2005 Jasper was sentenced to up to four years in an Idaho prison for heroin and methamphetamine possession charges. When released from prison in 2008, Jasper had only a high school education. Over the next ten years, he stayed clean and went back to school. In 2016 he earned a doctorate in clinical psychology from George Fox University in Newberg, Oregon. Today forty-nine-year-old Jasper lives in Oregon, where he hopes to use his degree to help others struggling with substance abuse problems. His felony drug conviction was a barrier to achieving his goals, so Jasper applied for a pardon. "My end goal, my hope is to become a licensed psychologist in the state of Oregon. The probability of me attaining my license with a felony record is very low," Jasper wrote in his application to Idaho's Commission of Pardons and Parole. "I am seeking a pardon in order to achieve my goal of becoming a licensed professional and to permanently break the destructive cycle of my past."[6]

In 2018 Idaho governor Butch Otter granted Jasper's pardon. While it does not erase his criminal record, it makes it easier for Jasper to achieve his goals. "Mr. Jasper is an example of why a pardon process exists in Idaho," says Sandy Jones, the commission's executive director. "He demonstrates how rehabilitation can and should work. He has worked hard to change his life through recovery and education, and the commissioners are pleased to support his pardon."[7]

For many other drug offenders, the outcomes are not as positive. According to a 2018 study conducted by the Bureau of Justice Statistics, drug offenders were highly likely to reoffend. The study followed inmates from state prisons for nine years, starting at their release in 2005. Researchers found that the recidivism rate—the likelihood that someone who broke the law once will do it again after being set free—for drug offenders was 42.8 percent in the first year after release. Over nine years, 83.8 percent of released drug offenders were arrested again for another offense.

RECEIVING & RELEASE

ATTENTION
DELIVER IN... PROPERTY TO R&R
PROPERTY C... ...OVER PROPERTY.

ATTENTION
DO NOT UNLOAD YOUR VEHICLE WITHOUT
AUTHORIZATION FROM R&R STAFF.

ATTENTION
DELIVER INMATE MONIES, C-FILES
MEDICAL FILES TO INTAKE PODIUM

Inmates await processing at a California prison that offers vocational education. Some drug offenders have turned their lives around with the help of programs like this one while others cycle in and out of prison.

Jason Wasylenko, a thirty-two-year-old from Falls Township, Pennsylvania, cycled in and out of prison while he struggled with an addiction to heroin. Since 2003 Wasylenko has spent a total of about eleven years in prison for drug-related crimes. As a teen, Wasylenko experimented with marijuana and prescription drugs. After his father's death, he tried heroin and quickly became hooked. Soon he would do anything to get his next fix and avoid withdrawal symptoms. At first he stole from retail stores to fund his addiction. When that was not enough, he started selling drugs. Off and on, Wasylenko tried to get clean, but he always relapsed. Eventually he was arrested in 2003 and sent to jail for the first time. Since that first arrest, Wasylenko has been in and out of jail four times, all for drug-related charges. With limited access to

In the United States drug laws and sentencing requirements have produced unequal outcomes for people of color. Countrywide, rates of drug use and sales are similar across races and ethnic groups. According to a 2016 report by the Hamilton Project, an economic policy initiative at the Brookings Institution, black and white Americans use and sell drugs at similar rates. However, black Americans are 2.7 times more likely to be arrested for drug-related crimes. Black Americans are also more likely to be convicted of drug crimes and serve longer sentences than white Americans. An investigation of sentencing disparities in Florida conducted by the *Sarasota Herald-Tribune* in 2016 found that African American defendants received prison terms that were twice the length or more of those received by white defendants for the same crimes under the same circumstances. For example, the investigation found that in Manatee County, judges sentenced white defendants convicted of felony drug possession to an average of five months in prison. Black defendants convicted of the same charges received more than a year behind bars.

addiction treatment and rehabilitation services in prison, many inmates like Wasylenko return to using drugs once released. Often they commit new crimes that send them back to prison.

Barriers to Success

After drug offenders and other inmates are released from prison, there are thousands of legal restrictions that severely restrict their ability to rebuild their lives, in the name of protecting public safety. These restrictions limit access to employment, housing, voting, and other opportunities. Former inmates may have difficulty finding a place to live if landlords refuse to rent to them or they do not have the money to pay for housing. For example, in Washington, DC, a person with a criminal record cannot receive housing vouchers, which help low-income people afford decent and safe housing.

People with a criminal record may also be barred from applying for certain jobs or obtaining professional licenses. In Wyoming former inmates are not permitted to hold certain county and municipal offices. In Missouri former inmates are not allowed to work for a state agency, while in Louisiana former felons may not become registered nurses. In some cases they are barred from performing jobs for which they received vocational training while in prison, such as barbering, plumbing, and electrical trades.

These barriers can have a significant negative impact on a drug offender's ability to reintegrate into society and become a law-abiding citizen after being released from prison. Like many drug offenders, Casey Irwin found it difficult to rebuild her life outside prison after serving seven years for drug charges. Her criminal record prevented her from getting affordable housing. She worked several low-wage jobs, but her lack of a high school

Voters in Virginia wait to cast their ballots. Once released from prison, many drug offenders face difficulty rejoining society because of restrictions that affect jobs, housing, and voting.

FEMALE DRUG OFFENDERS

Across the United States the number of women incarcerated is growing fast. According to a 2018 report from the Sentencing Project, from 1980 to 2016 the number of women serving time in federal and state prisons and jails skyrocketed from 26,378 to 213,772. This represents an increase of more than 700 percent. Many of these women are incarcerated for drug crimes. The percentage of women in prison for drug crimes has increased from 12 percent in 1986 to 25 percent in 2016, according to the Sentencing Project report.

Several factors have contributed to there being more women in prison. One is a shift in policing and enforcement practices to focus on low-level drug offenses such as possession. While both men and women have been affected by this change in focus, women are more likely than men to commit this type of drug offense.

Campbell County Jail in Jacksboro, Tennessee, offers one example of this change. More than a decade ago, there were rarely more than ten women in the jail at any given time. In 2018 the typical number of female inmates was sixty. Most were there on drug-related charges—and, according to a news media profile of the jail, many of the women are addicted to drugs. While in jail, these inmates receive little to no drug counseling to help with their addiction. As a result, many return to the jail as repeat offenders.

diploma and her criminal history made it difficult for her to find a job that paid the rent and provided for her two children. After a few years of struggling to make ends meet, Irwin turned to selling drugs to make quick money. Although she had participated in a drug treatment program in prison, it did little to help her survive in the outside world. So she returned to the drug world she knew. In 2014 Irwin was rearrested and sent back to prison for more than a year for drug possession. "The first time I went to prison, I didn't learn anything about myself, I was just surviving," Irwin says. "No one talked about behavior

"The first time I went to prison, I didn't learn anything about myself, I was just surviving."[8]

—Casey Irwin, convicted drug offender

change or why I was making those decisions I was making. I didn't have anybody forcing me to take a look at myself."[8]

For many former inmates like Irwin, these restrictions on where they can live and work make it extremely difficult to start over and stay out of trouble. "We're failing people returning to our communities from prison," says Christopher Wright Durocher, director of policy development and programming for the American Constitution Society. "To the extent that we pay attention to returning community members, we are focused on further punishing and isolating them, all but guaranteeing that they will again come in contact with the criminal justice system."[9]

USING PUNISHMENT TO DETER DRUG CRIMES

For many years, the predominant view in the United States was that long prison sentences were the best way to deter drug crime and use. The Anti-Drug Abuse Act of 1986 was built on this foundation. It established mandatory minimum sentences for many drug crimes. Before this law, the maximum federal penalty a person could receive for possessing any amount of any drug was one year in prison. After the act, offenses that involved certain quantities of drugs, such as 100 grams of heroin or 500 grams of cocaine, received five-year mandatory minimum sentences. A few years later new federal legislation imposed a mandatory minimum sentence for simply possessing even small amounts of crack cocaine, even if there was no evidence the offender intended to sell the drug.

Tough Drug Laws and Punishments

Since 1986 several states and the federal government have passed tougher drug laws that expand mandatory minimum sentences and lengthen prison sentences for drug crimes. In the 1990s several states and the federal government passed three-strikes laws. These laws required a person found guilty of committing a severe violent felony who had two other previous convictions to serve a mandatory life sentence in prison. These laws were intended to increase the punishment given to those convicted of more than two serious crimes. As of 2019 twenty-eight states—including California, Florida, Montana, New Jersey, and

Washington—had some type of three-strikes law. Although these laws were not aimed specifically at drug offenders, many drug offenders got caught in their widely cast net.

In addition, several states passed truth in sentencing laws. These laws were enacted to reduce the possibility that an inmate could be released early from prison. The laws required offenders to serve a significant portion of their sentence before they could be considered for release. Most truth in sentencing laws require inmates to serve 85 percent of their original sentence before they can be eligible for release.

The thinking behind these harsh laws and punishments is that people should be held accountable for their actions and that the threat of longer sentences would deter future drug crime. Supporters of harsh drug laws also believe that they send a public message that using illicit drugs is not acceptable in society and that those who choose to do so will be punished. "As a cultural matter, the US is dedicated to the idea of individualism—that people are accountable for their actions,"[10] says Christopher Slobogin, director of the criminal justice program at Vanderbilt University in Tennessee. These laws hold people accountable for their choices to use drugs and commit drug-related crimes. While people in other countries might look at crime, including drug crime, as the result of a situation or a set of circumstances, Americans tend to see crime as the result of poor decisions, explains Slobogin.

"As a cultural matter, the US is dedicated to the idea of individualism—that people are accountable for their actions."[10]

—Christopher Slobogin, director of the criminal justice program at Vanderbilt University in Tennessee

The movement toward harsher laws and punishments for drug crimes came during the height of the country's war on drugs. The war on drugs began in the 1970s as an effort to fight illegal drug use by significantly increasing penalties, enforcement, and incarceration for drug offenders. For example, in 1980 federal courts sentenced 26 percent of drug offenders

Under a 1986 law, possession of a certain amount of cocaine (shown) could lead to a mandatory minimum sentence of five years in prison.

to probation, which kept them out of prison, according to the Pew Charitable Trusts. By 2014 probation sentences for drug offenses had almost disappeared, with only 6 percent of federal offenders receiving probation.

As a result of these laws, the number of offenders incarcerated in America's prisons and jails rose from approximately 500,000 in 1980 to almost 2.3 million in 2018. The United States has the world's highest incarceration rate, putting 698 people behind bars for every 100,000 residents in 2018, according to a June 2018 report from the Prison Policy Initiative. The report's authors write:

> For four decades, the U.S. has been engaged in a globally unprecedented experiment to make every part of its criminal justice system more expansive and more punitive.

As a result, incarceration has become the nation's default response to crime, with, for example, 70 percent of convictions resulting in confinement—far more than other developed nations with comparable crime rates.[11]

Many of the inmates in US prisons are serving time for drug crimes.

Changing Policies

Under President Barack Obama, the federal government's approach to drug crimes changed course. Instead of increasing enforcement and sentencing for drug crimes, Obama and his attorney general, Eric Holder Jr., favored a mix of sentencing and rehabilitation for drug offenders, since they believed that a combination of the two was the most effective deterrent for future drug crime. In 2013 Holder encouraged federal prosecutors to use their discretion and consider individual circumstances in charging drug crimes. Holder's policy directed prosecutors not to report the amount of drugs in an arrest if doing so would trigger mandatory minimum sentencing for nonviolent offenders who were not part of a drug cartel or gang and did not sell drugs to children. At the time, Holder explained that he believed his policy was needed to reduce the prison population and more appropriately deal with nonviolent drug offenders. "With an outsized, unnecessarily large prison population, we need to ensure that incarceration is used to punish, deter, and rehabilitate—not merely to warehouse and forget,"[12] he said.

The federal government changed course again on drug crimes in 2017 when Donald Trump became president. His attorney general, Jeff Sessions, was a firm believer in stiff penalties for drug and other crimes. Citing a rise in violence in big cities and the increasing problem of opioid addiction across the country, Sessions called for a return to being tough on crime. He rolled back Holder's policy of letting prosecutors use their discretion in charging drug crimes and instead urged federal prosecutors to pursue the toughest charges that carried the harshest sentences in these cases. Sessions explained his position, writing in the *Washington Post*:

> While the federal government softened its approach to drug enforcement, drug abuse and violent crime surged. The availability of dangerous drugs is up, the price has dropped and the purity is at dangerously high levels. . . . My fear is that this surge in violent crime is not a "blip," but the start of a dangerous new trend—one that puts at risk the hard-won gains that have made our country a safer place. . . . Those of us who are responsible for promoting public safety cannot sit back while any American communities are ravaged by crime and violence. . . . Our new, time-tested policy empowers police and prosecutors to save lives.[13]

Supporters of tougher punishments for drug crimes praised Sessions's policy. The National Association of Assistant US Attorneys stated support of the policy. "The new guidance announced by Attorney General Sessions will restore the tools that Congress intended Assistant U.S. Attorneys to have at their disposal to prosecute drug traffickers and dismantle drug trafficking enterprises,"[14] the group said.

However, others disagreed, including Brett Tolman, a former US attorney for Utah under President George W. Bush and President Barack Obama. He argued that requiring harsher punishments and mandatory minimum sentencing without any consideration of individual circumstances could lead to unfair and overly harsh convictions. As an example, Tolman points to a case in which a pregnant woman drove a friend's car across the country without realizing it contained a secret compartment filled with methamphetamine. Police discovered the drugs and arrested the woman in Utah. Even though she did not have a criminal history

During his time as attorney general, Jeff Sessions (pictured) called for stiff penalties for drug crimes. He contended that a softened stance toward drug enforcement and penalties led to a surge in drug abuse.

and had no knowledge or involvement with the drug operation she unknowingly helped, the woman received a mandatory sentence of more than ten years in prison. "That's exorbitant,"[15] Tolman says.

Tough Punishment Can Work but Has Limits

Some research supports the idea that tough punishment and longer sentences can deter drug crime. The idea here is that people contemplating committing a crime will weigh the cost of the crime against its potential gain. *Cost* in this case refers to the likelihood of being caught and the severity of the punishment (with a longer prison sentence representing a higher cost). *Gain* refers to the hoped-for outcome of the crime (for instance, money taken

MANDATORY MINIMUMS

A mandatory minimum sentence is a minimum number of years that must be served when a person is convicted of a particular crime. Typically, mandatory minimum sentences range from five to ten years in prison. For drug crimes, mandatory minimum sentences are often based on the amount and type of drugs involved in a crime. Different drugs have different quantities that require a mandatory minimum sentence. For example, a first-time drug offender convicted of possessing 1 gram of LSD would receive a mandatory minimum sentence of five years in federal prison without parole. If convicted of possessing 10 grams of LSD, the first-time offender would receive a mandatory minimum sentence of ten years without parole. Mandatory minimum sentencing was implemented to punish high-level drug offenders. However, many lower-level drug dealers and users have also been convicted and sentenced under mandatory minimum sentencing laws.

during a theft). If people believe they are very likely to get caught and then receive a long prison sentence for little gain, they might decide not to commit the crime.

A study by researchers at the University of Essex and the University of Western Ontario concluded that harsh punishments do deter crime but only up to a certain point. In their study, the researchers followed a group of released prisoners in Italy. Because of Italian policy reform, some prisoners were released from prison early. Their freedom came with one condition: if they were caught breaking the law again, their unserved sentence would be added to their new sentence. This created a way for the researchers to measure how the people reacted to lighter or harsher sentences (depending on how much would be added to a new sentence). Individuals who had a long time remaining on their unserved sentence would face harsher punishment than those who had little unserved time left on their first sentence. The researchers used this information, along with recidivism rates, to track whether the threat of a harsher sentence acted as a deterrent to crime. The increased sentence lengths acted as a strong deterrent initially; however, the longer the sentence, the less of a deterrent it was. "Our estimates suggest that while increased sentence length can have quite strong deterrent effects for low initial sentence lengths, the incremental effects are much smaller for longer sentence lengths,"[16] write the researchers.

The researchers also suggest that instead of increased prison sentences, other law enforcement policies may be more effective at deterring crime. For example, investing in police forces through additional officers, equipment, and training may allow police to solve more crimes and apprehend more criminals. Increasing the likelihood a criminal will get caught and punished may deter him or her from committing the crime in the first place. "From a deterrence perspective," the researchers point out, "it might be beneficial to trade off the costs of incarceration associated with long prison sentences with policies aimed at increasing the certainty of punishment either through a higher probability of apprehension or through improved efficiency of the criminal justice system."[17]

Little Effect for Drug Crimes

While harsh punishments may have a deterrent effect on many crimes, other research has found that for drug crimes in particular, incarceration and the threat of longer sentences have little effect. A 2017 report by the Pew Charitable Trusts found that sending more people to prison for drug offenses has no effect on drug use, drug arrests, or overdose deaths. In the Pew report, the researchers studied state data on imprisonment, drug use, drug arrests, and overdoses. If harsh penalties deterred drug crime, then the researchers expected that the states with the harshest penalties (measured by the highest incarceration rates) would have the lowest rates of drug use. Instead, the researchers found no relationship between harsh penalties and reduced drug use, arrests, or overdoses. For example, although Louisiana had the highest incarceration rate and thus the harshest punishments, it ranked in the middle of studied states for overdoses, drug use, and drug arrests. In another example, Tennessee imprisons drug offenders at more than three times the rate of New Jersey, but the two states have almost identical rates of drug use.

According to Adam Gelb, the director of Pew's public safety performance project, these findings show that creating policies to toughen drug laws and punishments does little to deter people from using or selling drugs. "There seems to be this assumption that tougher penalties will send a stronger message and deter people from involvement with drugs. This is not borne out by the data,"[18] Gelb says.

"There seems to be this assumption that tougher penalties will send a stronger message and deter people from involvement with drugs. This is not borne out by the data."[18]

—Adam Gelb, the director of the Pew Charitable Trusts public safety performance project

Incarceration and Addiction

In recent years, more people are beginning to question whether harsher punishments are the best way to deal with drug crimes. As research has shown, many people who are arrested for drug crimes are also dealing with substance abuse and addiction. Simply locking them up in prison does little to address addiction issues and the reasons why they started using drugs in the first place. Richard J. Pocker, a former US attorney for Nevada, says:

> If we've learned anything during the 40-year war on drugs, it's that addiction can't be solved by incarceration, no matter how long. . . . From my years of experience in prosecuting criminals, I have learned that high incarceration alone is ineffective at controlling crime—particularly in the war on drugs. After more than 40 years of attempting to use a criminal justice solution to this public health problem, we have already learned that the threat of incarceration—no matter how harsh—does not deter people with a chemi-

cal addiction. They need treatment, not handcuffs. Our country is now in the midst of an opioid epidemic. With a record number of Americans dying every year from drug overdoses, we simply cannot afford to repeat the mistakes of our past.[19]

Substance abuse experts agree that incarceration alone is not the answer to reducing drug crime. Ed Gogek is an addiction psychiatrist who has worked for years in jails, prisons, homeless

High on meth and opioid pain meds, a woman waits in a Tennessee holding cell after being booked for drug possession. Research shows that prison does little to address problems linked to addiction.

clinics, and drug treatment programs. In his experience many inmates are arrested for something they did while under the influence of drugs or alcohol. Most have never had treatment for a substance abuse problem. "Prisons aren't just filled with criminals; they're filled with untreated substance abusers. If we could get them all into treatment and recovery, crime would drop dramatically,"[20] he says.

Still, Gogek believes that harsh drug laws and the threat of prison time are a necessary part of helping many drug offenders. "Tough drug laws save a lot of lives because the threat of jail keeps people in recovery,"[21] says Gogek. Most substance abus-

SERVING A LIFE TERM

Nearly two thousand federal inmates are serving life sentences for nonviolent drug offenses, according to a 2017 report from the Sentencing Project. Criminals convicted of drug trafficking can receive life sentences for dealing large quantities of drugs. The federal definition of a large quantity can be as small as a kilogram of heroin, a quarter kilogram of crack cocaine, or half a kilogram of a mixture of methamphetamine. Drug offenders can also be sentenced to life in prison if they have a significant criminal record or if prosecutors demonstrate that injury or death resulted from the drug's use.

Chris Young is serving time in federal prison for drug crimes. In 2010 federal law enforcement rounded up about thirty residents of Clarksville, Tennessee, involved in buying and selling powder cocaine and crack cocaine. According to the judge in the case, the arrests involved several low-level drug dealers handling small quantities of drugs, one of which was twenty-two-year-old Young. After Young was found guilty of drug trafficking of powder cocaine and crack cocaine, the prosecution filed for sentencing enhancements because of Young's two prior low-level drug convictions. The enhancements required a life sentence. In 2014 a judge sentenced Young to a mandatory life sentence.

ers do not think they have a problem and will not voluntarily seek treatment, he explains. If only offered treatment, most addicted offenders, Gogek believes, will fail to stay clean. He has seen countless inmates relapse back to using drugs, commit other crimes, and go back to prison. Gogek argues that the threat of prison gives drug offenders more incentive to participate in and complete treatment. "I've seen lots of people get clean and sober because they were facing possible prison time," he says. "I've seen people go to drug court insisting they would use drugs again as soon as the year was over, but halfway through realized they liked being clean and sober. I've had patients tell me getting arrested was the best thing that ever happened to them."[22]

"Tough drug laws save a lot of lives because the threat of jail keeps people in recovery."[21]

—Ed Gogek, addiction psychiatrist

DRUG TREATMENT AND REHABILITATION PROGRAMS IN PRISON

Mark's substance abuse problems started in his early teens. After taking his first drink of alcohol at age thirteen, he began binge drinking. Later he moved on to marijuana, Percocet, and finally heroin. By age twenty-two, he was hooked on drugs. On one occasion, after snorting drugs alone in a motel room, Mark passed out on the floor. As he lay there unconscious, the position his body was in slowly cut off the circulation to his right leg. By the time he was found, his leg needed to be amputated. In the hospital, Mark took advantage of the opiate painkillers doctors offered and continued using them after his release. He stole from his mother to fund his drug habit, until she finally reported him to the police. Since then, Mark has continued to struggle with his addiction and has been in and out of jail for drug-related crimes. Each time he was released, he returned to using drugs.

In 2017 Mark returned to prison in Rhode Island. This time, he hopes his outcome will be different. Mark is participating in the Rhode Island Department of Corrections' medication-assisted treatment program, one of the country's newest prison-based rehabilitation programs for drug offenders. Every day, Mark takes the addiction medication Suboxone under the supervision of a nurse. "Within 48 hours I felt like my old self, before I was even taking drugs," he says. "It makes me feel comfortable in my own skin."[23]

Treating Addiction Behind Bars

Many people in prison for drug crimes and other drug-related offenses are also dealing with a substance abuse disorder. According to the most recent study by the National Center on Addiction and Substance Abuse, approximately two-thirds of the 2.3 million inmates in the United States are addicted to drugs or alcohol. For many of them their drug addiction was a factor in their crime. Some were arrested and charged with the possession or sale of an illicit drug. Others took part in a theft or burglary or some other crime either under the influence of drugs or to get money to fund their drug habit, or both. Without treatment for their addiction, many of these inmates are at risk of reoffending and returning to prison within a few years of release. According to ProjectKnow.com, an online addiction resource of the American Addiction Centers, "It should come as no surprise to learn that a vast majority of addicts return to using after [being] released from jail. After all, locking people up doesn't solve the problem—it just buys a little time before they relapse, re-offend and perpetuate the endless cycle."[24]

Recognizing the need to treat inmates' substance abuse disorders before they are released into the community, some prisons have implemented addiction treatment programs. The types of treatment programs vary by prison and can include individual and group therapy, support group meetings, and drug education classes.

Some prison addiction programs use cognitive behavioral therapy to treat inmates. Cognitive behavioral therapy is a type of talk therapy that helps inmates identify negative thinking so they can challenge those thoughts and situations and respond to them in a healthy way. In federal prisons inmates can participate in a twelve-week cognitive behavioral therapy program that meets in group sessions with other inmates. The sessions focus on helping inmates recognize the types of situations that trigger their drug use. The inmates also learn skills to help them with communication, rational thinking, and adjustment once they leave prison.

Since its inception in 2015, the Kenton County Detention Center's substance abuse program has been popular with inmates. About 125 of the 700 inmates at the Kentucky jail are part of the program, and 60 more are on the waiting list. The program creates a community for inmates who are trying to break their addictions. Inmate Kenny Eva has been in jail for fourteen months on drug trafficking charges. On his first try, he dropped out of the program because he was not ready to make a change in his life. "The first time I'd say I didn't really get it yet. I wasn't ready, I was still trying to figure things out," says Eva. When he was ready, Eva rejoined the program. He says that three months later, he

Participants in a Colorado drug counseling and treatment program listen to another inmate as he tells prison authorities why he should be able to take part in the program.

was learning a lot. "Willing to be honest with yourself, being honest with yourself, open mindedness, being able to listen to other people,"[25] he says.

In North Carolina, drug possession was the number one crime sending people to prison in 2017. The majority of these drug offenders also struggle with addiction. A screening of all North Carolina inmates in 2017 found that 71 percent needed long-term substance abuse treatment. To help these inmates, the state offers Alcoholism and Chemical Dependency Programs. Program length can range from intermediate (ninety days) to long term (four to twelve months). The programs include cognitive behavioral therapy, activities to support a substance-free lifestyle, and individual and group counseling. Many "people entering prison have an alcohol or drug use problem that needs treatment," says Wrenn Rivenbark, clinical director of Alcoholism and Chemical Dependency Programs. "Our counselors provide that [treatment] through our evidence-based education and programming. We try to change thinking in order to change behavior."[26]

> "[Many] people entering prison have an alcohol or drug use problem that needs treatment. Our counselors provide that [treatment] through our evidence-based education and programming. We try to change thinking in order to change behavior."[26]
>
> —Wrenn Rivenbark, Alcoholism and Chemical Dependency Programs clinical director

Therapeutic Communities

For more intensive treatment, some prisons have established therapeutic communities for addiction treatment. In a therapeutic community, participants live together in a group setting away from the rest of the prison population. They participate in group meetings, counseling sessions, classes, seminars, and other group activities. Participants practice personal reflection and learn to take responsibility for their actions. They encourage each other to stay clean and not use drugs. The members of the community support each other as they navigate their recovery. The goal of a therapeutic community is to help participants adjust their thinking patterns so they will change their behavior and become law-abiding citizens once they are released from prison and return to the outside community. "Everything we do in therapeutic communities reflects real life," says Al Lopez, a correctional program manager in Washington State's Department of Corrections Substance Abuse Treatment Unit. "We want them to stop and think about their behaviors and think about what core skills to use to address the issue."[27]

Intensive therapeutic communities have been found to be one of the most effective types of drug treatment and rehabilitation programs in prisons. According to the Federal Bureau of Prisons, its Residential Drug Abuse Program (RDAP) reduces recidivism by approximately 16 percent for male inmates and 18 percent for female inmates.

Bridie Clevenger has taken part in one of these programs. She believes she now has the tools to turn her life around. Clevenger was only nine years old when she started using drugs. They helped her dull the pain of abuse and sexual assault she experienced at the hands of family members. Hooked on drugs as an adult, she stole money to fund her addiction and eventually was arrested and sent to prison. Now forty-four years old, Clevenger is part of a therapeutic community in a Washington state prison. She recently completed her last level of treatment and was scheduled for release. She planned to return to school and become a substance abuse counselor. "I want to give back what I was given," Clevenger says. "The person I am now is the person I've wanted to be for so long. I've learned today not to live in the wreckage of my past, or have it around my neck like an anchor. I live in the hope of the future, and I have to tell you that nothing has ever been brighter."[28]

Medication-Assisted Treatment

For years, treating drug addiction primarily involved group and individual therapy and support meetings. However, the growing opioid epidemic is changing how addiction is treated, both in and out of prison. Opioids are a class of drugs that act on the nervous system to relieve pain. These drugs are extremely addictive because they create artificial endorphins in the brain, which create warm, good feelings. Over time the user's brain stops producing these endorphins naturally. Using the drug is the only way the opioid addict can feel good. Without the drug, the user feels sick and depressed. By this point, the addict needs to take the drug—not to feel good—but simply not to feel bad. When the addict stops taking opioids, he or she experiences withdrawal symptoms such as anxiety, suicidal thoughts, depression, restlessness, sleep

REENTERING SOCIETY

Upon release from prison, former inmates face many barriers to successfully reentering society. Legal restrictions often limit where they can live and work. To help inmates transition back to society, some prisons offer reentry services, which have been shown to lower recidivism. Exodus House, a reentry program in Oklahoma, has helped keep former inmates out of prison. Over seven years only 13 percent of participants in the program have returned to prison.

Harold Sylvester is participating in a reentry program in Louisiana. He is a former drug dealer and addict who has been in and out of prison. Most recently, Sylvester spent four years in Lafayette Parish Correctional Center. Now he spends part of his day on work release getting job experience and returns to prison at night. He is hopeful that this time he will be able to rebuild his life.

problems, and more. Because of these symptoms, the likelihood that the addict will return to using is high. Opioid addiction has become a huge problem nationwide. Public health experts estimate that more than 2 million people have abused or become dependent on prescription and illegal opioid drugs, according to a 2019 CNN report.

Because opioid addictions are so difficult to break, many addiction and health professionals recommend medication-assisted treatment (MAT) programs. MAT is the use of approved medications, along with counseling and behavioral therapies, to treat opioid addiction. Use of these medications as part of a treatment program has been shown to be a more effective way of helping people stop using drugs and stay out of trouble than counseling programs alone.

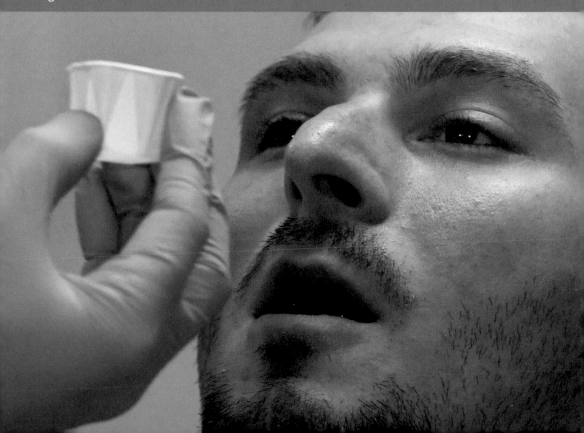

Under a medication-assisted treatment program, a Massachusetts prisoner receives his daily dose of buprenorphine. The drug helps to control opioid cravings.

A few prisons have implemented MAT programs for addicted inmates. Inmate George Ballentine is one of the lucky ones. Under the supervision of a nurse and two corrections officers, he receives a daily dose of buprenorphine. The drug, commonly known by the brand name Suboxone, controls his heroin and opioid cravings. Each day, Ballentine crushes the medication, places it under his tongue for fifteen minutes to dissolve, and then rinses his mouth and spits in a sink. "Suboxone for me is literally a Band-Aid," he says. "When you get a cut, what do you do? You put a Band-Aid on until it heals enough to take it off."[29]

Still, many prisons have been reluctant to use addiction medications. According to a 2018 Pew Charitable Trusts report, less than 1 percent of the nation's prisons and jails provide inmates with the available addiction medications approved by the US Food and Drug Administration (FDA), even though medical professionals and addiction experts support their use. Sometimes prison staff view using these medications as simply replacing one drug with another. Others note that the medications are costly. At the Franklin County Jail in Greenfield, Massachusetts, it costs about $12,500 per inmate per year for buprenorphine treatment. In addition, there are additional staff costs for services that are critical to the program, such as screening inmates, administering medication, providing counseling, and performing postrelease case management. "This is not a magic pill," says Ed Hayes, an assistant superintendent at the Franklin County Sheriff's Office. "It works only when these other elements are in place."[30]

Support for Medication-Assisted Treatment Grows

However, as newer medications and more evidence supporting the use of addiction medications have emerged, resistance to using them in prisons is decreasing. Nearly three hundred of the nation's prisons and jails now offer inmates an injection of naltrexone (also known as Vivitrol), a medication used to manage opioid dependence. Only about thirty facilities offer two of the

AFTERCARE PROGRAMS

More than half of inmates with addiction disorders relapse within a month of release from prison. Often their drug tolerance has lessened while they were in prison. That means they are more likely to experience a fatal drug overdose shortly after release. While completing prison-based drug rehabilitation can help inmates overcome addiction, the addition of aftercare services can improve outcomes even further. Aftercare programs provide outpatient rehabilitation care and twelve-step programs such as Narcotics Anonymous and Alcoholics Anonymous. These programs provide support to former inmates recovering from addiction and give them an opportunity to learn from people with similar issues.

other approved opioid addiction medications—methadone and buprenorphine. These medications are used to treat opioid addiction and lessen the symptoms of opioid withdrawal. However, according to criminal justice analyst Andrew Klein, who tracks MAT programs, the number of prisons offering inmate opioid addiction medication is growing.

Rhode Island's prisons offer some of the most comprehensive MAT programs in the United States. Every inmate entering the state's prison system is screened for an opioid addiction. Those who have a dependence on the drug are offered drug counseling along with all three FDA-approved drugs to treat addiction—methadone, buprenorphine, and naltrexone. Early indicators are that the program is succeeding. According to a study by researchers from Brown University, opioid overdose deaths dropped by nearly two-thirds among recently incarcerated people in Rhode Island. In addition to reducing overdose deaths after inmates are released, the program also increased the likelihood the offenders will stay in treatment after their release from prison and avoid being arrested again.

Inmates like Ballentine believe MAT is giving them a chance to start their lives fresh. Before his arrest Ballentine overdosed three times in three months. Before MAT he planned to resume using heroin when he was released from jail. Nine months later, he was released from jail with a new attitude and a determination to stay out of trouble. "The staff here decided not to give up on me even when I decided that I wasn't worth it," he says. After his release, Ballentine checked with his parole officer, picked up his buprenorphine prescription at a local pharmacy, and moved into a halfway house near the jail. His doctor believes that Ballentine will be ready to wean off the medication soon. "I feel like I'm ready for it," Ballentine says. He plans to volunteer at a soup kitchen and join in activities with other recovering addicts. "I've got backup plan after backup plan. I know it's no guarantee of success, but I'm doing everything possible."[31]

Difficult to Rehabilitate in Prison

Even with prison-based drug treatment and rehabilitation programs, recidivism rates are still high for drug offenders. According to a 2018 report from the Bureau of Justice Statistics, 83.8 percent of drug offenders were rearrested within nine years of release from state prison. These numbers suggest that prison-based rehabilitation programs are not as effective as they need to be. "Obviously what we're doing isn't working or we'd see greater reduction in recidivism rates and we wouldn't see a lot of these people going through the same issues," says Kelli Callahan, a criminal justice faculty member at American Military University. Callahan has worked in corrections for ten years, including two years in a correctional facility treatment unit. "Our inclination in corrections is to punish and that typically comes in the form of incarceration. When individuals are in prison, they're not going to get the same kind of ongoing rehabilitation needed to overcome their drug dependencies,"[32] she says.

"Our inclination in corrections is to punish and that typically comes in the form of incarceration. When individuals are in prison, they're not going to get the same kind of ongoing rehabilitation needed to overcome their drug dependencies."[32]

—Kelli Callahan, a criminal justice faculty member at American Military University

Florida drug offenders celebrate their graduation from a jail life skills program. The woman on the right will go to a halfway house, where she will receive continued support as she tries to rebuild her life.

There are a variety of reasons why prison-based treatment and rehabilitation programs are not experiencing better outcomes. To start, access to effective programs is often limited. While many state prisons have drug rehabilitation programs, many county jails do not. Inmates who serve time in a jail may have to wait until they get to a state prison before they are eligible for treatment. Even once they are in a prison with a program, the waiting list to receive treatment may be long. Often inmates with shorter sentences may be given priority for placement in drug treatment programs because they will be released sooner. As a result, inmates with longer sentences may find that they have to wait, sometimes for years, until a spot opens up in the program. Even when they do enter a program, many of these programs still do not have adequate MAT available, which makes it more likely opioid addicts will relapse.

In some rehabilitation programs, inmates complete their treatment and then return to the general prison population. Drug offenders who have begun to make progress dealing with their addiction and life choices are forced to live and interact with other inmates who have not undergone similar changes in attitude and behavior. "I have someone on my unit that has five years left— why send them back to general population?" says Frank, a prison drug counselor in New York. "When you put them back in [general population], anything that you've gained you lose because you're with people who know nothing about treatment."[33] Seth Ferranti, who served more than twenty years in federal prison, agrees. While in prison, Ferranti completed a ten-month RDAP. "RDAP worked like this: you finished the program, graduated, and went to [a] halfway house, so you took the program at the door," says Ferranti. "That is how it should work because it is counterproductive to put someone who just went through the program back in a harmful environment that can lead to relapse."[34]

Sometimes prison-based rehabilitation programs do not work simply because the inmate does not want to get better and turn his or her life around. When drug treatment is court mandated or forced on an inmate, chances of success are often slim. "I got a good experience out of the program because I wanted to come back to society," says Ferranti. "I wanted to be prepared but prison is a hard place to carry that type of attitude. I had been in a long time and prisoners respected me so I could carry it how I wanted but someone fresh into prison and trying to change is going to have a hard time with all the peer pressure and politics."[35]

Other times, prison-based programs have mediocre outcomes because the wrong inmates are placed in the program. In some states, drug treatment programs are mandated for anyone convicted of a drug crime, regardless of whether the inmate has

"I got a good experience out of the program because I wanted to come back to society. I wanted to be prepared but prison is a hard place to carry that type of attitude."[35]

—Seth Ferranti, convicted drug offender

a drug problem. When the inmate is serving time for selling drugs but does not have a substance abuse problem, drug treatment and addiction-focused rehabilitation programs have no meaning or benefit.

Many people incarcerated for drug crimes are also struggling with addiction. Without treatment, these people are at risk of returning to drugs and committing crimes that will send them back to prison. Prison-based addiction treatment programs offer some hope of breaking this cycle of addiction and incarceration.

Chapter 4

ALTERNATIVE SENTENCING PROGRAMS

Decades of tough-on-crime legislation and harsh sentencing practices led to a surge in people incarcerated for drug crimes. According to a 2018 report from the Sentencing Project, the number of people incarcerated for drug crimes dramatically increased from 40,900 in 1980 to 450,345 in 2016. Harsh sentencing laws, including mandatory minimum sentences, have kept many people convicted of drug crimes incarcerated for longer periods. In 1986 a person serving time for a federal drug offense spent an average of twenty-two months in prison. By 2004 a person convicted of the same drug offense was likely to serve sixty-two months behind bars, almost tripling the sentence. Most of these people are not major players in drug trafficking, and many have no prior history of violent crime.

The increase in people serving time for drug crimes has left state and federal prisons struggling to deal with overcrowded prisons and limited funding. Without enough space, staff, and funding to deal with greater numbers of inmates, prisons often cut back on educational and treatment programs that drug offenders need for rehabilitation. Also, prison conditions suffer as staff struggle to keep up with general maintenance and sanitation. Fewer staff to watch larger numbers of inmates in close quarters also increases the likelihood of violent incidents between inmates and guards.

In Idaho drug offenders make up an increasing share of inmates in the state's overcrowded prisons. Approximately one-fifth

of the state's prison population is behind bars for drug possession convictions, according to the Idaho Department of Correc-
tion (IDOC). Many of them are prior offenders who had been released on parole or given probation sentences. "The vast majority
of individuals serving time on drug possession charges are viola-
tors of probation or parole prior to coming to prison,"[36] says IDOC
spokesperson Jeff Ray.

Evaluating Punishment-Based Justice

As the United States faces a growing overcrowding problem in
its prisons, more people are calling for criminal justice reform to
reduce harsh laws and sentencing, particularly for nonviolent offenders, which includes many drug offenders. Critics of harsh
punishment-based justice systems point out that there is little evidence that lengthy incarcerations reduce crime rates. Additionally, when drug offenders are sent to prison, the punishment-based
justice system continues to fail them by not providing adequate
programs and policies to ensure that they can reenter society
as productive and law-abiding citizens. Kevin Kempf, the executive director of the Association of State Correctional Administra-
tors and a former director at IDOC, believes that the prison overcrowding problems that many states are dealing with could be
relieved by reevaluating how the criminal justice system handles
people convicted of drug crimes. "The state of Idaho needs to
look at who is being sent to prison. People that are selling, manu-
facturing drugs, in my opinion, those people do
need to spend time in prison," Kempf says.
Drug users, on the other hand, are being
punished for being addicts. He adds,
"Prison doesn't make them better. It
makes them worse."[37]

> "People that are selling,
> manufacturing drugs, in
> my opinion, those people
> do need to spend time in
> prison."[37]
>
> —Kevin Kempf, executive director of
> the Association of State Correctional
> Administrators

To explore the effectiveness of
prison time in curbing drug abuse and
crime, researchers from the Pew Charitable Trusts analyzed data from federal

A gymnasium has been turned into living space for inmates at an overcrowded California prison. Alternative sentencing programs for nonviolent drug offenders are one way to address this problem.

and state law enforcement, corrections departments, and health agencies. They found that although the number of inmates imprisoned for drug crimes increased significantly from 1980 to 2015, there was no statistically significant effect on three indicators of drug problems: self-reported drug use, drug overdose deaths, and drug arrests. The results contradict the claims of punishment supporters, that stiff prison sentences deter drug use and crimes. "The evidence strongly suggests that policymakers should pursue alternative strategies that research shows work better and cost less,"[38] write the report's authors.

Research has also shown that reducing prison terms for certain drug offenders has not led to higher rates of reoffending. In 2007 the US Sentencing Commission retroactively reduced the sentences of thousands of crack cocaine offenders. A study that

POSTPRISON EDUCATION

Keith Whiteman first went to prison for drugs in 1995, at age twenty. Over the next two decades, he returned to prison many times, stuck in a cycle of serving time behind bars, getting out for a few months, committing another offense, and returning to prison. It was all connected to his addiction to drugs. While in prison, Whiteman tried every treatment program the prison had to offer, but his problems with drugs, addiction, and crime continued. "Prison wasn't the solution," said Whiteman in an interview for a 2018 film about addiction and incarceration, *Sentencing Reform: Drug Addiction*.

Then in 2008 Whiteman joined the Post-Prison Education Program right before his release from prison. The program helped him reenter the community. Counselors provided housing, groceries, transportation, and other basic needs. Most importantly, they mentored Whiteman intensively as he tried to regain his life. For the first time Whiteman had people who cared about his success, and that gave him hope that he could change. With their support, Whiteman was able to overcome his addiction, earn a college degree, and enter a career in human services.

Quoted in Ari Kohn, "Drug Addiction Isn't a Crime—We Just Treat It like One," *Nation*, April 12, 2018. www.thenation .com.

followed the offenders for the next seven years found that the offenders who had their sentences shortened had no higher rate of rearrest than those who did not have their sentences shortened.

Alternative Sentencing Programs

Incarceration is appropriate for some drug offenders, experts say. But for others—in particular, addicts who commit nonviolent crimes to support their habit or who have been convicted of possessing small amounts of illegal drugs—other options have been shown to have better outcomes. Alternative sentencing programs give drug offenders with addiction problems the opportunity to participate in rehabilitation-focused programs instead of going to prison. Offenders who satisfactorily complete the program may avoid a conviction on their record. Common alternative sentencing programs for drug offenders include diversion programs that require a person to participate in a structured rehabilitation and treatment program, addiction treatment, psychological counseling, and educational programs.

Alternative sentencing programs are based on the belief that rehabilitation is more effective than incarceration for certain drug offenders. These programs recognize that the key to preventing these offenders from committing more crimes in the future is to treat their underlying addiction. Without treatment for addiction, offenders are likely to return to drug use and crime. For many drug offenders, alternative sentencing programs are the best chance to participate in professional, supervised rehabilitation. Such programs give drug offenders the opportunity to turn their lives around, instead of serving time in prison without appropriate treatment for their addiction.

Not every drug offender is eligible for alternative sentencing programs. A person who has committed a violent offense would not qualify. The individual must not have a prior criminal record, either. And he or she must complete an evaluation and demonstrate a willingness to fully embrace rehabilitation. If an offender is determined eligible for an alternative sentencing program, a judge may order the offender to be diverted into a treatment program instead of being sent to prison.

Alternative sentencing in Ohio gave a young man named Taylor the opportunity to break his heroin addiction and turn his life around. When Taylor was in his early twenties, he and a few friends tried painkillers to get high. At first, Taylor had no trouble getting more prescription pain pills. Soon he was not just using them for fun. He was addicted. But then new laws made it harder to get the pills. Scarcity increased the price, so Taylor turned to a cheaper alternative: heroin. His addiction grew, and then he lost his job and moved in with his father. The drug use continued, and eventually Taylor's father reported to police that his son had stolen his car. After police arrested Taylor and confirmed his drug use, a judge offered the young man a chance to participate in an alternative sentencing program. Instead of going to jail, Taylor spent thirty days in the Community Alternative Sentencing Center. The program included substance abuse treatment, mental health services, and educational and vocational services. "I decided to really invest myself and get everything I could from this program," Taylor says. "I wanted tools and accountability."[39] After the thirty days, Taylor was able to move directly into a recovery home, where residents live and support each other. Today Taylor still receives counseling and attends Narcotics Anonymous meetings. He is looking forward to getting back to work.

Reforms in Georgia

Various states are creating their own versions of alternative sentencing programs. Authorities in Georgia, for example, decided in 2012 that sending nonviolent drug offenders to prison was not beneficial to the offenders or the state. The state decided to take a more rehabilitation-focused approach to dealing with drug crimes and other nonviolent crimes. Lawmakers restructured sentences for drug and property crimes. Lawmakers came up with alternative sentencing options to hold offenders accountable and reduce the likelihood that they would commit future crimes. These alternative sentencing options included substance abuse treatment and accountability courts. By reserving incarceration for the state's most serious criminals, public safety improved and criminal justice costs decreased. Newt Gingrich and Kelly McCutchen wrote in 2017:

> Georgia's story is an incredible one for many reasons. First, it disproves the widely held belief that incarcerating more offenders means less crime. The reforms in Texas and Georgia—as well as South Carolina, Mississippi and other states—show alternatives can be more effective. Second, it shows that being "tough on crime" by incarcerating offenders for long sentences—and for every offense,

large or small—is more about playing politics than getting results. The research tells us that long sentences for low-level, nonviolent offenders can result in worse public safety outcomes. Housing lower-risk people with more danger-ous offenders makes them more dangerous themselves. In this way, harsh sentences make our streets less safe.[40]

Participants in the state's alternative sentencing programs say these programs are working. In April 2018 six participants from Georgia's Ocmulgee Judicial Circuit's Adult Treatment Court

A Louisiana inmate studies car repair in a prison auto shop. Research shows that job training, education, counseling, and addiction treatment result in better outcomes for addicted drug offenders.

WISE WORKS

In Wise County, Virginia, an alternative sentencing program called Wise Works is putting people convicted of nonviolent felonies, usually drug crimes, to work in the community instead of sending them to prison. The offenders do all types of odd jobs, from painting lines on the Little League field to helping out at the local animal shelter. They do not get paid for their work; instead, they are working off their drug charges.

For twenty-nine-year-old Jessie Shuler, Wise Works has been a much better alternative than prison. After high school, Shuler became addicted to painkillers. When she was deep in her addiction, she wrote and cashed checks in her father's name to pay for her drugs. Even though she got into treatment and was no longer on drugs, years later Shuler still had an outstanding warrant for her arrest for check fraud, grand larceny, and prescription fraud. Shuler took a plea deal and joined Wise Works. Instead of going to prison, she was sentenced to 1,440 hours of work without pay. It took nine months of full-time work to complete her sentence, but Shuler says it was worth it. She got to be at home with her infant son and not miss any of his milestones.

Collaborative (ATCC) celebrated an important milestone. After eighteen to twenty-four months of the intensive rehabilitation program, the six former drug abusers graduated from the diversion program and moved closer to long-term recovery.

The ATCC program has been an effective alternative to jail time for these and other nonviolent offenders. Entry into this program is at the discretion of judges. Beyond treating drug addiction, the program helps participants find housing and a job and get an education. Participants receive individual and group counseling to deal with their addiction and mental health issues. They take life skills and high school equivalency courses (if they did not finish high school) and participate in employment counseling. While in the program, they are subject to drug screenings and curfews, and they attend twelve-step meetings. James Lanthrip III, one of the April graduates, completed the program after battling drug addiction for seventeen years. He plans to join the ATCC as a peer counselor. Says Lanthrip:

> I'm anxious to help somebody else, I really am. Today I have tools—I don't have to go back out in the world and use. Those days are behind me, and if that thought process ever does cross my head, I've got goals that I can look back at that I've achieved through this process. I have people in my support system that I can call that will stop what they're doing to come and help me, and I'll stop what I'm doing to help any participant in here, too. It's a good feeling.[41]

Law Enforcement Efforts

Another type of alternative sentencing program, the Law Enforcement Assisted Diversion (LEAD) program, is being used in Seattle, Washington. LEAD gives police officers the option to send repeat nonviolent offenders to social service programs instead of criminal courts. Introduced in 2011, LEAD aims to break the cycle of arrest and incarceration often experienced by drug offenders. Under the LEAD program, a police officer who stops someone for certain types of offenses, including low-level drug crimes, can decide whether to send the offender into the criminal justice system or directly to a social service worker who will arrange drug treatment, housing, and other rehabilitative services.

The LEAD program targets people with a long history of drug use, but it is not for everyone. People who are caught with more than 3 grams of illegal drugs do not qualify. People who have felony convictions for serious violent crimes or who are suspected of promoting prostitution or exploiting minors also cannot take part in this program. Once

"Today I have tools—I don't have to go back out in the world and use. Those days are behind me, and if that thought process ever does cross my head, I've got goals that I can look back at that I've achieved through this process."[41]

—James Lanthrip III, diversion program graduate

in the program, however, participants are assigned caseworkers who can provide immediate help with getting a hot meal and a safe place to sleep. Caseworkers also help participants get into drug treatment programs and find stable housing and job training.

LEAD coordinators expect that some participants will relapse. Unlike many other diversion programs, this one will give participants a second chance if that happens. According to

A participant in Seattle's LEAD program (foreground) shops for groceries and other items with his caseworker. This program aims to break the cycle of arrest and incarceration often experienced by drug offenders.

Lisa Daugaard, policy director of the Public Defender Association in Seattle, the overall goal of the program is to give repeat drug offenders the ability to turn their lives around and stay out of the justice system. If an offender successfully completes the recommended treatment and services, no criminal charges are filed.

The LEAD program has been a big part of Johnny Bousquet's recovery. Since his early teens, Bousquet was in and out of trouble with drugs and the law. In 2014 the thirty-seven-year-old was taken into custody for drug dealing. He said that he had reached the point that "I didn't want to die, but I didn't want to live."[42] Instead of sending him to prison, police referred Bousquet to LEAD. The program got him into drug treatment, found him housing, and bought him essentials like shoes and toothpaste. Bousquet says he has been drug-free in the months since he joined LEAD. He is looking forward to the future and hopes to pursue a career in music and writing. Case manager Mikel Kowalcyk says he believes that LEAD has helped Bousquet turn his life around. "He is going to make it,"[43] says Kowalcyk.

Bousquet is one of many who have benefited from the LEAD program. A University of Washington study compared arrest data for participants and nonparticipants (or control group) in the LEAD program. The researchers found that LEAD participants had a 58 percent lower likelihood of arrest compared with the control group. LEAD participants were also 39 percent less likely to be charged with a felony than the other individuals. "The analysis always showed that, compared to the control group, the LEAD program seemed to have a positive effect on arrests,"[44] says Susan Collins, University of Washington associate professor and co-author of the LEAD study.

Because of the program's success, LEAD has been replicated in twenty cities across the country, and more are being developed. Santa Fe, New Mexico, launched its own version of the LEAD program in 2014. A 2018 review compared the number of arrests in the six months before and six months after participants entered the program. That review found a 30 percent decrease in new arrests during that period. In addition, participants reported reduced use of heroin and improved quality of life. "The data shows that diversion programs that stop arresting people for drug possession improve health outcomes, without compromising public safety," says Emily Kaltenbach, New Mexico state director for the Drug Policy Alliance. "Treating people in the health system instead of punishing them in the criminal justice system leads to better outcomes for individuals as well as the community at large."[45]

"The data shows that diversion programs that stop arresting people for drug possession improve health outcomes, without compromising public safety."[45]

—Emily Kaltenbach, New Mexico state director for the Drug Policy Alliance

DRUG COURTS

Kaitlyn Smith graduated from a Florida drug court program in January 2017. Now twenty-seven, she remains drug-free and healthy. "I owe my recovery to drug court," says Smith. "It saved my life."[46] Her life looked to be on a very different path in 2014 when police officers pulled her over and searched her car. Inside they found her sleeping infant and a variety of drugs, including sleeping pills and cocaine. She was arrested and charged with three felony counts of drug possession.

When Smith appeared in court, the judge gave her a choice—go to jail or enter drug court. Smith knew she needed help. She had started using painkillers in 2012 after a car accident. She developed an addiction and after a while began experimenting with other drugs. She lost touch with family and friends, and her health worsened. Her only interest was where and when she would get her next fix.

That day before the judge, Smith chose to enter drug court. She spent three years in the drug court program, receiving treatment for her addiction. During that time, her physical and mental health improved significantly. At the time of her arrest, Smith thought it was the worst day of her life. Now, she describes it as the best. "I am so thankful I was arrested that day," she says. "If that didn't happen, I wouldn't be alive today."[47]

What Are Drug Courts?

Drug courts are programs within state or county court systems created specifically to deal with nonviolent, mostly first-time offenders who have a drug problem. The country's first drug courts were established in 1989 in Florida's Miami-Dade County. The main goal of drug courts is to reduce substance use and keep participants from committing new crimes that could send them to prison. Drug courts combine treatment with sanctions, allowing offenders with drug problems to get the help they desperately need. Individuals in drug court are usually facing charges of drug possession or sale or drug-related crimes such as theft. Those who are given a chance to go through drug court must demonstrate a strong desire to get help with their addiction and turn their life around.

Today there are more than three thousand drug courts across the United States. Instead of being incarcerated, eligible offenders who have pleaded guilty to low-level, nonviolent drug crimes can go through treatment, counseling, and other rehabilitative services. Many drug courts require participants to find a job or perform volunteer work while in the program. Drug court programs typically last from six months to a few years. Participants must adhere to strict requirements. They must remain drug-free and agree to monitoring and weekly drug testing. They must participate in counseling sessions and twelve-step meetings. They must regularly appear before a judge, who reviews their progress, noting whether they have been attending counseling, passing drug tests, looking for work, and meeting other requirements. Failure to adhere to the rules of the program, such as failing a drug test, can lead to sanctions. A judge might issue a warning or order the participant to spend a few days in jail. Judges can also revoke participation in drug court if participants repeatedly break program rules. This action usually results in prison time for the original charges that landed the individuals in drug court in the first place.

Douglas Smith experienced this firsthand in 2018. Smith was facing several drug-related felony charges in Jefferson County, New York. He was offered the opportunity to go through drug court. If he completed the program, his charges would be reduced to misdemeanors, and he would not have to serve addi-

A drug court participant speaks with a judge in a Michigan courtroom. Drug court judges monitor the participant's progress and adherence to all program requirements.

tional time in county jail. After twice failing to fulfill his obligations in the program, Smith was kicked out of the program and ordered to county jail to serve out the full sentence on the original charges.

When participants successfully complete a drug court program, the court may dismiss the charges against them. This keeps the crime off their criminal record so that it will not impair their ability to get a job, loan, or housing. According the Chris Deutsch, director of communications for the National Association of Drug Court Professionals (NADCP), drug courts provide an effective way to fight recidivism. "We have tried to incarcerate our way out of problems," says Deutsch. "But what we saw was that people who don't get treatment will continue to use and reoffend."[48] Deutsch notes that drug court may not be appropriate for low-level drug offenders who do not have substance addictions, since they will not benefit from the treatment required by the court.

> "We have tried to incarcerate our way out of problems. But what we saw was that people who don't get treatment will continue to use and reoffend."[48]
>
> —Chris Deutsch, director of communications for the NADCP

Phases of Rehabilitation

Most drug court programs include three or four phases of rehabilitation. Providers assess each participant and create an individual rehabilitation plan that addresses the person's needs. First, the participant may need to be stabilized. The stabilization phase often involves detoxification from drugs and alcohol and may also include treatment for medical or psychological disorders. Next, participants begin the second stage of intensive treatment. This phase can last for several months to a year. During this phase, participants receive substance abuse treatment and counseling. They may also be offered education and help finding a job. Some programs require participants to find and hold a job during the program. Status hearings with the judge also occur during the intensive treatment phase. The final phase is transition, which supports participants as they learn to stay sober and out of trouble while the court's supervision lessens.

These various stages of rehab can—and do—help people rebuild their lives. After an arrest for forgery, Donna Boggs was given the chance to enter a Kansas drug court. Over the years, the fifty-two-year-old drug addict had been in and out of jail because of crimes related to her addiction. During the ten-month program, Boggs completed several phases. In the first thirty-day phase, she attended counseling and kept a calendar to make sure she did not miss any upcoming court dates or counseling sessions. Over the next sixty days, Boggs attended individual counseling and Narcotics Anonymous meetings. She also actively searched for a job. In the final phase, Boggs continue with the required tasks from earlier phases, such as treatment, court appointments, and twelve-step meetings. She also learned life skills to prepare her for living clean and crime-free after drug court. After ten months with no relapses, Boggs was eligible to graduate from drug court. "As the person moves through the program and demonstrates that they are going to their meetings and engaging in treatment, they may appear less frequently in court," says Deutsch. "There is always a degree of monitoring, but it gets less intensive as they progress toward graduation."[49]

NOT EFFECTIVE FOR EVERYONE

Not everyone who participates in drug court is a success story. After overdosing on heroin and being arrested in 2016, Joshua Smith was given the chance to go through an Arizona drug court instead of being sent to jail. Smith pleaded guilty to a drug-related felony and entered the program. He had tried unsuccessfully many times to break his opioid addiction. Like many opioid addicts, Smith realized that he needed medical help to quit using opioids. He needed medication-assisted treatment (MAT) in order to detox and prevent a relapse. However, the Arizona drug court program banned the use of MAT, even if a doctor ordered it. Unable to use the addiction medication, Smith relapsed. He tested positive for opioids at a drug court screening and was sanctioned with a sixty-day jail sentence. His mother's request for the court to reconsider its policy on MAT was denied. Without access to addiction medication, Smith faces an uphill battle to overcome his drug addiction and avoid future drug crimes.

Helping Many in Madison County

Over the years, drug courts have helped thousands of drug offenders avoid incarceration and get their lives back on track. The
Madison County drug court in Kentucky is one of these. It has
helped dozens of drug offenders since it began in 1998. To qualify for the county's drug court, offenders must sign a document
that states that they committed the crime for which they were
charged. If participants do not complete their obligations in drug
court, the signed confession can be used against them in court. If
a participant completes drug court, the charge is dismissed. After

A graduate of a West Virginia drug court (right) receives a congratulatory hug
from his probation officer as the smiling judge looks on. Court supervision
decreases as the offender nears graduation.

sixty days, the charge can be expunged, which legally erases it from a person's criminal record. Judge Jean Chenault Logue presides over the Madison County drug court. She believes drug court is a good option when a person has committed a crime that is too serious for probation but would not benefit from time in prison.

Like many drug courts across the country, the Madison County drug court program is a lot of work for participants. It begins with a multiple-session orientation. Each participant is assigned different weekly requirements, which could include drug testing, counseling, curfews, and more. Participants also work toward goals such as getting a general equivalency diploma or developing job skills by performing community service. All participants work to become drug-free and report regularly to the court for monitoring. It takes an average of two years to complete the Madison County program.

Tabitha Roark is a former Madison County drug court participant who now works for the court providing peer support. When she was still a participant, a typical day began with a phone call to find out whether she needed to undergo a drug test that day. If yes, she reported to the office to perform the test. Then she would go to work, attend twelve-step meetings, and return home before curfew.

Every other week, the drug court team meets to discuss each participant's progress in the program. The participants appear before the court to talk about what they are doing and what is expected of them. For both officials and participants, drug court can be an emotional roller coaster. It can be difficult to watch participants fail. However, when they succeed, it is very rewarding. "Graduation is very exciting and also makes me nervous," says Logue. "Now we are letting go. You want people to succeed."[50]

The Kentucky results show that drug courts are succeeding. According to the latest evaluation in 2015, two years after drug court graduation no graduates were in state prisons, and only 28 percent were in local jails. That contrasts with 81 percent of nonparticipants who were in prison or jail two years after serving their sentences. "It's not 100 percent effective," says Logue. "But I will say, we have a lot of success."[51]

A Vital Component of Justice Reform

The success of drug courts has led to these programs operating in every state and territory in the United States. According to the NADCP, participants in drug court programs are six times

VETERANS COURTS

Nicholas Stefanovic completed tours of duty in Iraq and Afghanistan for the US Marine Corps from 2002 to 2006. During that time, the horrors of war affected his mental health. Upon his return to the United States, Stefanovic struggled with nightmares, anger, and panic attacks. He began to use prescription opioids to deal with his post-traumatic stress disorder. Eventually, Stefanovic developed an opioid addiction. He was arrested in 2009 for attempting to cash stolen checks. Instead of going to prison, the former marine was given the chance to participate in Rochester Veterans Court in New York. Veterans court is a type of drug court that specializes in dealing with military veterans with substance abuse problems who have committed a crime. These courts help veterans improve mental health, reduce substance use, and stay out of jail.

Veterans courts often work in partnership with local veterans organizations and facilities. As of 2017, there were more than three hundred veterans courts in the United States. Thanks to veterans court, Stefanovic's mental health improved, the panic attacks became less frequent, and he stopped using drugs. The veterans court helped Stefanovic get his life back.

An Illinois drug court graduate who struggled for years with addiction now has a job and says that the program changed her life. Drug courts have been so successful that they are now found in every state in the country.

more likely to stay in treatment and improve their health. Numerous studies have shown that drug courts can reduce crime and substance use. After graduation, 75 percent of drug court participants remain arrest-free, as compared to 30 percent of offenders released from prison, according to the NADCP. Also, drug court participants demonstrate lower rates of substance use than non-participants. If they relapse, additional treatment is often shorter.

Drug courts help ease prison overcrowding and save the criminal justice system money. According to the NADCP, sending a person to drug court instead of state prison can save up to $13,000 per individual. In addition to saving money, drug courts free up criminal justice resources to deal with violent and other serious criminal cases. Staff and services can be directed toward offenders who are a greater risk to community safety. When prison space has been freed up by sending nonviolent drug offenders to drug court, the space can be used to incarcerate more dangerous offenders.

"Drug courts merge a public health approach into law enforcement interactions."[52]

—Jerome Adams, US surgeon general

Increasingly, drug courts are viewed as a vital component of criminal justice reform. In September 2018 the White House Office of National Drug Control Policy announced a two-year grant of $4 million for the NADCP. The grant will be used to fund training and technical assistance for drug courts nationwide. At a September 2018 roundtable discussion at the White House with NADCP leaders, drug court judges, and drug court graduates, US surgeon general Jerome Adams praised the grant and the work of drug courts. Adams said:

> I've seen first-hand the effectiveness of drug courts as they provide an array of recovery support services for those suffering from an addiction. Drug courts merge a public health approach into law enforcement interactions. The best drug courts set realistic standards, and help participants address education, job training and housing issues. This is what stigma reduction and cutting-edge public policy progress looks like.[52]

Drug crime is costly to society for individuals, communities, and the country as a whole. Understanding how to effectively deal with and reduce drug crime, whether it be punishment, rehabilitation, or a combination of the two, benefits everyone.

SOURCE NOTES

Introduction: Punish or Rehabilitate?

1. Quoted in Matt Ferner, "This Man Is Serving More than 13 Years in Prison over Two Joints' Worth of Marijuana," Huffington Post, September 9, 2015. www.huffingtonpost.com.
2. John Cornyn, "Cornyn: Texas Shows Criminal Justice Reform Works," John Cornyn United States Senator for Texas, December 18, 2018. www.cornyn.senate.gov.
3. Cornyn, "Cornyn."
4. Quoted in ACLU, "91 Percent of Americans Support Criminal Justice Reform, ACLU Polling Finds," November 16, 2017. www.aclu.org.

Chapter 1: Serving Time for Drug Crimes

5. Quoted in Jenny Wagner et al., "For Some Addicts, Jail Has Become De Facto Treatment," *U.S. News & World Report*, May 29, 2018. www.usnews.com.
6. Quoted in Cynthia Sewell, "Idaho Governor's 3rd-Ever Pardon Is a Drug Convict Devoting His Life to Mental Health," *Idaho Statesman* (Boise), April 13, 2018. www.idahostatesman.com.
7. Quoted in Sewell, "Idaho Governor's 3rd-Ever Pardon Is a Drug Convict Devoting His Life to Mental Health."
8. Quoted in Lottie Joiner, "When Twisted Justice Stops Prisoners from Starting Over," *USA Today*, June 19, 2017. www.usatoday.com.
9. Quoted in *USA Today*, "We Keep Pushing People Back into Prison," August 24, 2017. www.usatoday.com.

Chapter 2: Using Punishment to Deter Drug Crimes

10. Quoted in Bryan Lufkin, "The Myth Behind Long Prison Sentences," BBC, May 15, 2018. www.bbc.com.

11. Peter Wagner and Wendy Sawyer, "States of Incarceration: The Global Context 2018," Prison Policy Initiative, June 2018. www.prisonpolicy.org.

12. Quoted in Pete Williams, "Attorney General Sessions Orders Tougher Drug Crime Prosecutions," NBC News, May 12, 2017. www.nbcnews.com.

13. Jeff Sessions, "Jeff Sessions: Being Soft on Sentencing Means More Violent Crime. It's Time to Get Tough Again," *Washington Post*, June 16, 2017. www.washingtonpost.com.

14. Quoted in Jon Schuppe, "Attorney General Sessions Charts Course Back to Long Drug Sentences," NBC News, May 13, 2017. www.nbcnews.com.

15. Quoted in Schuppe, "Attorney General Sessions Charts Course Back to Long Drug Sentences."

16. Giovanni Mastrobuoni and David A. Rivers, "Criminal Discount Factors and Deterrence," February 7, 2016. https://papers.ssrn.com/sol3/papers.cfm?abstract_id=2730969.

17. Mastrobuoni and Rivers, "Criminal Discount Factors and Deterrence."

18. Quoted in Jon Schuppe, "Imprisoning Drug Users Doesn't Affect Use, Study Says," NBC News, June 20, 2017. www.nbcnews.com.

19. Richard J. Pocker, "Harsher Penalties Won't Solve Nation's Drug Problem," *USA Today*, July 14, 2017. www.usatoday.com.

20. Ed Gogek, "To Treat Drug Addiction, We'll Still Need Jail Time," *Newsweek*, November 10, 2015. www.newsweek.com.

21. Gogek, "To Treat Drug Addiction, We'll Still Need Jail Time."

22. Gogek, "To Treat Drug Addiction, We'll Still Need Jail Time."

Chapter 3: Drug Treatment and Rehabilitation Programs in Prison

23. Quoted in Beth Schwartzapfel, "A Better Way to Treat Addiction in Jail," Marshall Project, March 1, 2017. www.themarshallproject.org.

24. ProjectKnow.com, "Jail Fail: Locked Up Addicted, Released Addicted," 2019. www.projectknow.com.
25. Quoted in Ally Kraemer, "Jail's Substance Abuse Treatment Program in Kenton County in High Demand," WCPO, August 13, 2018. www.wcpo.com.
26. Quoted in Keith Acree, "Facilities Celebrate Successes," Addiction Professionals of North Carolina. www.apnc.org.
27. Quoted in Rachel Friederich, "Therapeutic Communities: 20 Years of Breaking the Cycle of Addiction," Department of Corrections Washington State, September 27, 2017. www.doc.wa.gov.
28. Quoted in Friederich, "Therapeutic Communities."
29. Quoted in Philip Marcelo, "Jails, Prisons Slowly Loosen Resistance to Addiction Meds," AP News, August 7, 2018. www.apnews.com.
30. Quoted in Marcelo, "Jails, Prisons Slowly Loosen Resistance to Addiction Meds."
31. Quoted in Marcelo, "Jails, Prisons Slowly Loosen Resistance to Addiction Meds."
32. Quoted in Jinnie Chua, "Ending the Cycle of Recidivism: Rehabilitating Non-Violent Drug Offenders," In Public Safety, April 13, 2018. https://inpublicsafety.com.
33. Quoted in Keri Blakinger, "8 Major Problems with Drug Treatment in Prison," Fix, December 1, 2015. www.thefix.com.
34. Quoted in Blakinger, "8 Major Problems with Drug Treatment in Prison."
35. Quoted in Blakinger, "8 Major Problems with Drug Treatment in Prison."

Chapter 4: Alternative Sentencing Programs

36. Quoted in Nicole Blanchard, "You Asked: Who Does Idaho Send to Prison? And What If We Sent Fewer People?," *Idaho Statesman* (Boise), October 3, 2018. www.idahostatesman.com.

37. Quoted in Blanchard, "You Asked."
38. Pew Charitable Trusts, "More Imprisonment Does Not Reduce State Drug Problems," March 8, 2018. www.pewtrusts.org.
39. Quoted in Greater Cincinnati Behavioral Health Services, "Back on Track—Alternative Sentencing Program Provides Valuable Insight," August 31, 2018. www.gcbhs.com.
40. Newt Gingrich and Kelly McCutchen, "Column: Criminal Sentencing Reform in Georgia Has Become National Model," *Augusta (GA) Chronicle*, November 18, 2017. https://csgjustice center.org.
41. Quoted in Will Woolever, "Local Residents Graduate from ATCC, Gain Tools to Succeed," *Milledgeville (GA) Union-Recorder*, April 19, 2018. www.unionrecorder.com.
42. Quoted in John R. Emshwiller and Gary Fields, "Seattle Police Chafe Under New Marching Orders," *Wall Street Journal*, December 30, 2014. www.wsj.com.
43. Quoted in Emshwiller and Fields, "Seattle Police Chafe Under New Marching Orders."
44. Quoted in Sara Jean Green, "LEAD Program for Low-Level Drug Criminals Sees Success," *Seattle Times*, April 8, 2015. www.seattletimes.com.
45. Quoted in Drug Policy Alliance, "New Data Shows Promise for Santa Fe's Innovative Law Enforcement Assisted Diversion (LEAD) Program," October 11, 2018. www.drugpolicy.org.

Chapter 5: Drug Courts

46. Quoted in Matt Gonzales, "Drug Courts in the United States," DrugRehab.com, June 12, 2017. www.drugrehab.com.
47. Quoted in Gonzales, "Drug Courts in the United States."
48. Quoted in Gonzales, "Drug Courts in the United States."
49. Quoted in Gonzales, "Drug Courts in the United States."

50. Quoted in Critley King, "Madison In-Depth: Sentencing Second Chances Through Drug Court," *Richmond (KY) Register*, September 28, 2018. www.richmondregister.com.
51. Quoted in King, "Madison In-Depth."
52. Quoted in White House, "ONDCP Announces Key Funding for Nation's Drug Courts," September 26, 2018. www.whitehouse.gov.

Drug Policy Alliance
131 W. Thirty-Third St., 15th Floor
New York, NY 10001
website: www.drugpolicy.org

The Drug Policy Alliance is a nonprofit organization that advocates for drug policy reform. Its website has information about the latest issues relating to the war on drug and criminal justice reform, as well as numerous fact sheets.

Marshall Project
156 W. Fifty-Sixth St., Suite 701
New York, NY 10019
website: www.themarshallproject.org

The Marshall Project is a nonprofit news organization covering the criminal justice system. Its website has many articles, profiles, and interviews about the criminal justice system, including several dealing with incarceration and drug offenders.

National Association of Drug Court Professionals (NADCP)
625 N. Washington St., Suite 212
Alexandria, VA 22314
website: www.nadcp.org

The NADCP is a training and advocacy organization for the treatment court model, which now includes over three thousand programs found in every state in the United States. Its website has information, fact sheets, and the latest news involving drug courts.

Prison Policy Initiative
PO Box 127
Northampton, MA 01061
website: www.prisonpolicy.org

The Prison Policy Initiative is a nonprofit organization that produces research about criminal justice and prison policies and advocates for a more just system. Its website has links to numerous research publications, including studies of incarceration and sentencing.

Sentencing Project
1705 DeSales St. NW, 8th Floor
Washington, DC 20036
website: www.sentencingproject.org

The Sentencing Project is a nonprofit organization that works to achieve a fair and effective criminal justice system by promoting sentencing reforms, addressing racial disparities, and advocating for incarceration alternatives. Its website offers many articles and fact sheets about the criminal justice system, including drug policy.

FOR FURTHER RESEARCH

Books

Nicole Horning, *Drug Abuse: Inside an American Epidemic*. Farmington Hills, MI: Lucent, 2018.

Nicole Horning, *Drug Trafficking: A Global Criminal Trade*. Farmington Hills, MI: Lucent, 2018.

Michael Kerrigan, *The War on Drugs*. Broomall, PA: Mason Crest, 2016.

Barbara Krasner, *Harm Reduction: Public Health Strategies*. Farmington Hills, MI: Greenhaven, 2019.

Clive Somerville, *Defending Our Nation: The Drug Enforcement Administration*. Broomall, PA: Mason Crest, 2017.

Internet Sources

Matt Gonzales, "Drug Courts in the United States," DrugRehab .com, June 12, 2017. www.drugrehab.com.

Jan Hoffman, "She Went to Jail for a Drug Relapse. Tough Love or Too Harsh?," *New York Times*, June 4, 2018. www.nytimes .com.

Pew Charitable Trusts, "More Imprisonment Does Not Reduce State Drug Problems," March 8, 2018. www.pewtrusts.org.

Wendy Sawyer and Peter Wagner, "Mass Incarceration: The Whole Pie 2019," Prison Policy Initiative, March 19, 2019. www .prisonpolicy.org.

Jon Schuppe, "As Drug Sentencing Debate Rages, 'Ridiculous' Sentences Persist," NBC News, May 2, 2016. www.nbcnews .com.

INDEX

PICTURE CREDITS

Cover: Shutterstock.com/iStockphoto

6: Associated Press

10: Associated Press

13: Associated Press

15: Rob Crandall/Shutterstock.com

20: photopixe/Shutterstock.com

23: Mark Reinstein/Shutterstock.com

27: Associated Press

32: Rick Wilking/Reuters/Newscom

36: Associated Press

40: St. Petersburg Times/Zuma Press/Newscom

45: Lucy Nicholson/Reuters/Newscom

49: Associated Press

52: Associated Press

57: Associated Press

60: Associated Press

63: Associated Press

ABOUT THE AUTHOR

Carla Mooney is the author of many books for young adults and children. She lives in Pittsburgh, Pennsylvania, with her husband and three children.